MLS 49

THE MOST EVER

by William Cole
illustrated by Mike Thaler

FRANKLIN WATTS | NEW YORK | LONDON | 1976

Library of Congress Cataloging in Publication Data

Cole, William, 1919–
    Knock knocks, the most ever.

    SUMMARY: A collection of "knock knock" jokes. 1.
        Wit and humor, Juvenile. [1. Joke books]
I. Thaler, Mike, 1936– II. Title.
PZ8.7.C58Kn   [398.6]   75–33205
ISBN 0–531–02428–8
ISBN 0–531–01142–9 lib. bdg.

101245

Knock knock.

Who's there?

Matthew.

Matthew who?

Matthew lace came untied.

Knock knock.

Who's there?

Wendy.

Wendy who?

Wendy moon comes over de mountain...

Knock knock.

Who's there?

Dwayne.

Dwayne who?

**Dwayne the tub!
I'm dwowning!**

Knock knock.

Who's there?

Harris.

Harris who?

Harris nice to have on the top of your head.

Knock knock.

Who's there?

Althea.

Althea who?

**Althea later,
alligator!**

Knock knock.

Who's there?

Justin.

Justin who?

Justin time for dinner!

Knock knock.

Who's there?

Nicholas.

Nicholas who?

A Nicholas not much money these days.

Knock knock.

Who's there?

Jess.

Jess who?

Jess me.

Knock knock.

Who's there?

Anastasia.

Anastasia who?

Anastasia wagon has four doors.

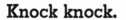

Knock knock.

    Who's there?

Wanda.

    Wanda who?

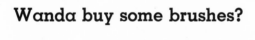

Wanda buy some brushes?

Knock knock.

Who's there?

Caesar.

Caesar who?

Caesar jolly good fellow,
Caesar jolly good fellow!

Knock knock.

Who's there?

Morris.

Morris who?

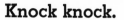

**Morris Friday.
The next day's Saturday.**

Knock knock.

    Who's there?

Philip.

    Philip who?

Philip the tank,
I've got a long way to go.

Knock knock.

Who's there?

Henrietta and Juliet.

Henrietta and Juliet who?

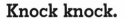

**Henrietta big dinner
and got sick. Juliet the same thing,
but she's okay.**

Knock knock.

Who's there?

Hyman.

Hyman who?

Hyman a terrible hurry!

Knock knock.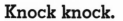

Who's there?

Yvonne.

Yvonne who?

Yvonne
to be
alone.

Knock knock.

Who's there?

Isaac.

Isaac who?

Isaac ... get me a doctor!

Knock knock.

Who's there?

Venice.

Venice who?

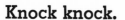

Venice you going
to open dis door?

Knock knock.

Who's there?

Fanny.

Fanny who?

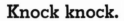

Fanny body calls, I'm out.

Knock knock.

Who's there?

Earle.

Earle who?

Earle be glad to put this down.

Knock knock.

Who's there?

Emmeline.

Emmeline who?

Emmeline! Wanna hear me roar?

Knock knock.

Who's there?

Amaryllis.

Amaryllis who?

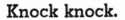

**Amaryllis state agent.
Wanna buy a house?**

Knock knock.

Who's there?

Harold.

Harold who?

Hark! the Harold angels sing.

Knock knock.

Who's there?

Ralph.

Ralph who?

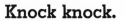

Ralph! Ralph! Ralph!
I'm your puppy dog!

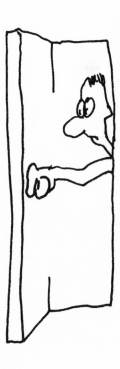

Knock knock.

　　Who's there?

Olga.

　　Olga who?

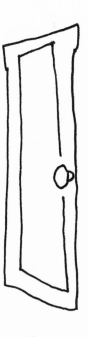

Olga home if you don't open up.

Knock knock.

Who's there?

Tennessee.

Tennessee who?

Tennessee you tonight?

Knock knock.

Who's there?

Ida.

Ida who?

Ida know why
I love you like I do . . .

Knock knock.

Who's there?

Heywood, Hugh, and Harry.

Heywood, Hugh, and Harry who?

Heywood, Hugh, Harry up and open this door?

Knock knock.

Who's there?

Barry.

Barry who?

Barry me not on
the lone prairie.

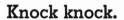

Knock knock.

Who's there?

Gladys.

Gladys who?

Gladys can be that you're home!

Knock knock.

Who's there?

Isabelle.

Isabelle who?

**Isabelle out of order?
I had to knock.**

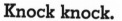

Knock knock.

Who's there?

Shelby.

Shelby who?

Shelby comin' round
the mountain
when she comes....

Knock knock.

    Who's there?

Meg.

    Meg who?

Meg the bed ... I wanna go to sleep.

Knock knock.

Who's there?

Ishmael.

Ishmael who?

Ishmael for you.

Knock knock.

Who's there?

Witch.

Witch who?

Witch way to Chicago?

Knock knock.

Who's there?

Ferdinand.

Ferdinand who?

Ferdinand
worth two
in the bush.

Knock knock.

Who's there?

John.

John who?

John the navy
and see the world.

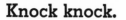

Knock knock.

Who's there?

Artichoke.

Artichoke who?

Artichoke when he swallowed his yo-yo.

Knock knock.

Who's there?

Celeste.

Celeste who?

Celeste time I'm gonna lend <u>you</u> money!

Knock knock.

Who's there?

Abie.

Abie who?

**Abie stung me
on the nose!**

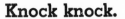

Knock knock.

　Who's there?

Ammon.

　Ammon who?

Ammon ole cowhand from the Rio Grande....

Knock knock.

Who's there?

Pollyanna.

Pollyanna who?

Pollyanna bad kid when you get to know her.

Knock knock.

Who's there?

Teresa.

Teresa who?

Teresa pretty tall around here.

Knock knock.

Who's there?

Eskimo.

Eskimo who?

Eskimo questions, I'll tell you no lies.

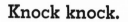

Knock knock.

Who's there?

Moppet.

Moppet who?

**Moppet up
before it
gets sticky.**

Knock knock.

Who's there?

Tilly.

Tilly who?

Tilly who?
What are you,
a fox hunter?

Knock knock.

Who's there?

Ahab.

Ahab who?

Ahab to go
to the
bathroom.

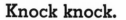

Knock knock.

Who's there?

Little old lady.

Little old lady who?

I didn't know
you could yodel!

Knock knock.

Who's there?

Oz.

Oz who?

Oz standin' here
waitin' for ya.

Knock knock.

Who's there?

Gorilla.

Gorilla who?

Gorilla me a hamburger.

Knock knock.

Who's there?

Adolph.

Adolph who?

**Adolph ball
hit me
in the mouf.**

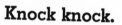

Knock knock.

Who's there?

Police.

Police who?

Police open up.
Thank you.

Knock knock.

Who's there?

Kojak.

Kojak who?

Kojak up the car.
I got a flat.

Knock knock.

Who's there?

Francis.

Francis who?

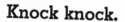

**Francis where
people speak French.**

Knock knock.

Who's there?

Saul.

Saul who?

Saul over town that you're in love with me ...

Knock knock.

Who's there?

Arkansas.

Arkansas who?

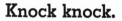

**Arkansas wood
better than you can.**

Knock knock.

> Who's there?

Sarah.

> Sarah who?

Sarah doctor in the house?

Knock knock.

Who's there?

Ken.

Ken who?

Ken I please come in?

Knock knock.

Who's there?

Lucinda.

Lucinda who?

Lucinda chain.
I wanna get in.

Knock knock.

Who's there?

Oswald.

Oswald who?

Oswald my chewing gum!

Knock knock.

Who's there?

Sibyl.

Sibyl who?

**Sibyl Simon
met a pieman ...**

Knock knock.

Who's there?

King Kong.

King Kong who?

King Kong
the witch
is dead....

Knock knock.

Who's there?

Howell.

Howell who?

**Howell I get in if you
don't open the door?**

Knock knock.

Who's there?

Marcella.

Marcella who?

Marcella's full of water.

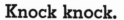

Knock knock.

Who's there?

Dinosaur.

Dinosaur who?

Dinosaur at you — you burned the toast.

Knock knock.

Who's there?

Ivan.

Ivan who?

Ivan standin' here ten minutes! Let me in!

Knock knock.

Who's there?

Murray Lee.

Murray Lee who?

Murray Lee
we roll along . . .

Knock knock.

Who's there?

Orson.

Orson who?

**Stop Orson around
and let me in!**

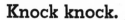

Knock knock.

Who's there?

Hubbard.

Hubbard who?

Hubbard can sing louder than his bird.

Knock knock.

Who's there?

Missouri.

Missouri who?

Missouri loves company.

Knock knock.

Who's there?

Carlotta.

Carlotta who?

Carlotta
trouble
when it
breaks down.

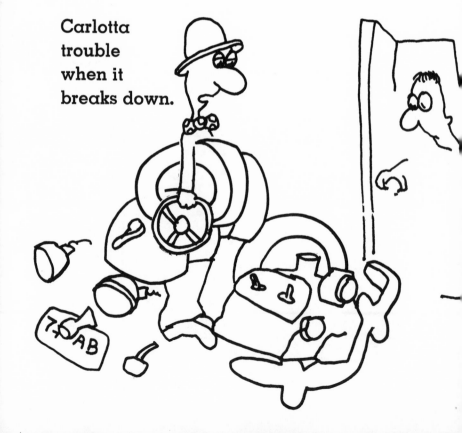

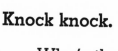

Knock knock.

Who's there?

Ira.

Ira who?

Ira sign!

MORE

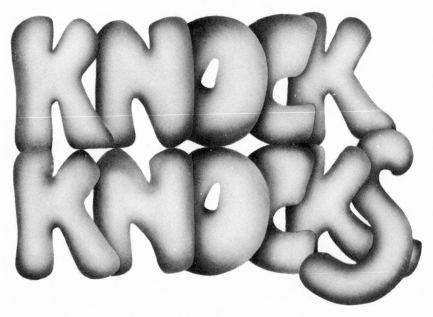

Knock knock.
    Who's there?
José.
    José who?
José can you see by the dawn's early light ...

Knock knock.
    Who's there?
Euripides.
    Euripides who?
Euripides pants, you'll pay for dem!

Knock knock.
    Who's there?
Hayden.
    Hayden who?
I'm Hayden this waitin' out here.

Knock knock.
    Who's there?
Oliver.
    Oliver who?
Oliver but she doesn't love me.

Knock knock.
    Who's there?
Lief.
    Lief who?
Lief me alone!

Knock knock.
    Who's there?
Harvey.
    Harvey who?
Harvey gonna play this game forever?

Knock knock.
    Who's there?
Isadore.
    Isadore who?
Isadore open or locked?

Knock knock.
    Who's there?
Sam.
    Sam who?
Sam person who knocked the last time.

Knock knock.
     Who's there?
Hammond.
     Hammond who?
Hammond cheese on rye, please.

Knock knock.
     Who's there?
Alice.
     Alice who?
Alice forgiven, please come home.

Knock knock.
     Who's there?
Danielle.
     Danielle who?
Danielle so loud, I can hear you!

Knock knock.
     Who's there?
Sigrid.
     Sigrid who?
Sigrid Service, open up!

Knock knock.
    Who's there?
Fido.
    Fido who?
Fido I have to wait out here?

Knock knock.
    Who's there?
Marcus Welby.
    Marcus Welby who?
Marcus Welby 'cause we need to pass.

Knock knock.
    Who's there?
Liza.
    Liza who?
Liza wrong to tell.

Knock knock.
    Who's there?
Angelo.
    Angelo who?
Angelo tastes good with whipped cream.

Knock knock.
    Who's there?
Oscar.
    Oscar who?
Oscar if she has a sister.

Knock knock.
    Who's there?
Sherwood.
    Sherwood who?
Sherwood like to get inside.

Knock knock.
    Who's there?
Estelle.
    Estelle who?
Estelle waitin' for you to open up.

Knock knock.
    Who's there?
Hobbit.
    Hobbit who?
Hobbit lettin' me in?

Knock knock.
    Who's there?
Rita.
    Rita who?
Rita good book, you'll feel better.

Knock knock.
    Who's there?
Maura.
    Maura who?
Maura see you, Maura like you.

Knock knock.
    Who's there?
Juno.
    Juno who?
I don't know, Juno?

Knock knock.
    Who's there?
Manny.
    Manny who?
Manny are called but few are chosen.

Knock knock.
    Who's there?
Hugh.
    Hugh who?
Hugh who yourself!

Knock knock.
    Who's there?
Consuelo.
    Consuelo who?
I Consuelo! My throat's sore.

Knock knock.
    Who's there?
Beth.
    Beth who?
Beth wishes, thweetie!

Brrrng brrrng.
    Who's there?
Hurd.
    Hurd who?
Hurd my hand, so I couldn't knock knock.

Knock knock.
    Who's there?
Avon.
    Avon who?
Avon to get in!

Knock knock.
    Who's there?
Homer.
    Homer who?
Is this your Homer your business?

Knock knock.
    Who's there?
Humphrey.
    Humphrey who?
Humphrey all!

Knock knock.
    Who's there?
Boo.
    Boo who?
Don't cry, you'll feel better tomorrow.

Knock knock.
> Who's there?

Gus.
> Gus who?

Gus who? That's what
you're supposed to do!

Knock knock.
> Who's there?

Juan.
> Juan who?

Juan of your good friends.

Knock knock.
> Who's there?

Noah.
> Noah who?

Noah yes! Which is it?

Knock knock.
> Who's there?

Anatole.
> Anatole who?

Anatole me you're a pain in the neck.

Knock knock.
        Who's there?
Harvey and Gunther.
        Harvey and Gunther who?
Harvey Gunther wait
around here all night?

Knock knock.
        Who's there?
Theodore.
        Theodore who?
Theodore wasn't open so I knocked.

Knock knock.
        Who's there?
Colleen.
        Colleen who?
Colleen up your room!

Knock knock.
        Who's there?
Hugo.
        Hugo who?
Hugo jump in the lake!

Knock knock.
> Who's there?

Tucson.
> Tucson who?

Tucson an' two daughters are enough kids.

Knock knock.
> Who's there?

Jerome.
> Jerome who?

Jerome on the range lately?

Knock knock.
> Who's there?

Cousin Mae.
> Cousin Mae who?

You're Cousin Mae a lot of trouble
these days!

Knock knock.
> Who's there?

Walter.
> Walter who?

Walter wall carpets are nice.

Knock knock.
    Who's there?
Gomez.
    Gomez who?
Gomez around with
somebody else, I'm busy.

Knock knock.
    Who's there?
Cynthia.
    Cynthia who?
Cynthia been gone, I mith you very much.

Knock knock.
    Who's there?
Sis.
    Sis who?
Sis anyway to treat a friend!

Knock knock.
    Who's there?
Abbot.
    Abbot who?
Abbot you're not as smart as I am.

Knock knock.
> Who 's there?

Butch, Jimmy, and Al.
> Butch, Jimmy, and Al who?

Butch your arms around me and
Jimmy a little kiss or Al go home.

Knock knock.
> Who's there?

Dishes.
> Dishes who?

Dishes the FBI — open up!

Knock knock.
> Who's there?

Alex.
> Alex who?

That's the last time Alex you for a favor!

Knock knock.
> Who's there?

Amos.
> Amos who?

A mosquito bit me on the ear.

Knock knock.
    Who's there?
Hosanna.
    Hosanna who?
Hosanna Claus gets down those chimneys
I'll never know!

Knock knock.
    Who's there?
Orange.
    Orange who?
Orange you glad school's out?

Knock knock.
    Who's there?
Howard.
    Howard who?
Howard you like a punch in the nose?

Knock knock.
    Who's there?
Hatch.
    Hatch who?
God bless you!

Knock knock.
    Who's there?
Andrew.
    Andrew who?
Andrew a picture of Mary
that hurt her feelings.

Knock knock.
    Who's there?
Leopold.
    Leopold who?
Leopold the class and
everyone wants a new teacher.

Knock knock.
    Who's there?
Tom.
    Tom who?
Tom on! You know who I am.

Knock knock.

    Who's there?

Sophie.

    Sophie who?

Sophie come to the end of the book!

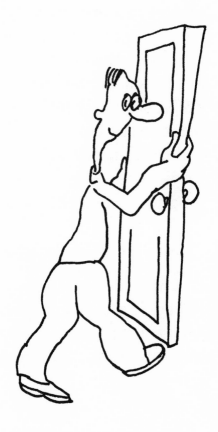

ABOUT THE AUTHOR

William Cole is a well-known anthologist, writer, and editor. He has created over forty anthologies and has written numerous books for children. Of **Knock Knocks: The Most Ever** he says, "I collected a few old favorites. Then I bought a paperback called **What Shall We Name the Baby?** and spent hours going over the names, mumbling to myself and testing jokes on children. The whole experience was a lot of fun and very interesting. I came to see that knock knocks stimulate a child's imagination and interest in the language. They are an introduction to punning and to the delights of English."

ABOUT THE ARTIST

Versatile, funny, and totally in tune with children, Mike Thaler is a cartoonist, teacher, sculptor, draftsman, and songwriter. To date, he has eighteen children's books to his credit. He is also the creator of the popular TV character Letterman, from **The Electric Company.** Of **Knock Knocks: The Most Ever** he says, "It's fun."

101245

DATE DUE

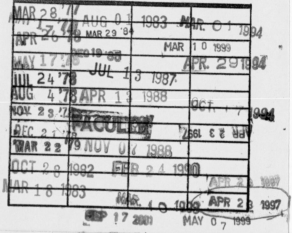